Laugh, Baby Sister

by Paula Morrow
Illustrations by Alice Sinkner

"Look at me, Hana!"

Kent danced in front of his baby sister. But Hana was watching Mama mash pears.

"Can I feed Hana?" asked Kent.

"No, thank you," said Mama.

Mama put a spoon full of pears in Hana's mouth. The baby rubbed some pears on her face.

"Can I wash Hana's face?" asked Kent.

"No, thank you," said Mama.

She washed Hana's face.
Kent wanted to help.

Mama put Hana in her baby swing. The phone rang. Mama reached for it. Hana started to cry.

"Oh dear," said Mama. "Kent, can you help Hana?"

Kent did a new dance for Hana.
But Hana just cried.

"Please stop crying," Kent said.

Kent made his funniest face.
Hana cried some more.
Kent wanted to make her laugh.

Kent reached for Hana's toy lamb.
He gave it to Hana.
Hana threw it on the floor.

"Oh, Hana!" said Kent.

"Poor lamb," said Kent, picking it up.
Then Kent had an idea.

Kent started to sing.

"Baa, baa, black sheep," he said.

Hana watched Kent.
Kent sang. He shook the toy to make it dance.
Soon Hana stopped crying.

Kent kept singing.
He made the lamb clap its feet.
Hana laughed and clapped her hands.
Mama finished talking on the phone.

"Kent, you are a good helper!" she said.

Then Kent and Mama sang the sheep song together.

Hana sang, too. She sang, "Baa, baa, baa!"